NOT BITTER,
BETTER

A Woman's Story on Overcoming the Odds While Healing Along the Way

Dr. Katrina R. Sparks

Publishing Services By: Pen Legacy Publishing
Editing & Formatting By: Carla M. Dean, U Can Mark My Word
Cover Design By: Christian Cuan
Front Cover Photos By: Lee Alexander Photography

Library of Congress Cataloguing – in- Publication Data has been applied for.

ISBN: 979-8-9872891-8-1

PRINTED IN THE UNITED STATES OF AMERICA.

First Edition

DEDICATION

This book is dedicated to my mother and son.

I AM because of you.

Thank you!

TABLE OF CONTENT

NOT BITTER,
BETTER

A Woman's Story on Overcoming the Odds While Healing Along the Way

INTRODUCTION

Generational curses! What exactly are they? Pastors, therapists, and even life coaches have stressed the need to break generational curses. As cliché as it may seem, we must address generational curses before they distress our lives. For me, breaking my family's curse happened all too late. You see, my mother was raised by her mother until the age of two and then by family members; my father was raised without his father, and the story you are reading was written by a child raised by a single mother and an inconsistent father. Then, I became a woman who raised my son with an absent father, thus making me a single mother! Do you see the pattern? While several families may have successfully broken the generational curses that engrained their venom, others are still falling victim. Instead of living a life of self-pity and blaming, we should learn our family's story so we can make better decisions for *our* story. Your grandmother may have carried the curse your mother didn't know how to break, but you are built and afforded the tools to finally put an end to it.

How many of you became victims of generational curses and living with the scars? How many of you are ready to break the chains? Before we get to work, let's examine what generational curses are and why they are so hard to break. Exodus 34:7 says, "Yet he does not leave the guilty unpunished; he punishes the children and their children for the sin of the parents to the third and fourth generation." According to The Gospel Coalition, "generational curse describes the cumulative effect on a person of things that their ancestors did, believed, or practiced in the past, and a consequence of an ancestor's actions, beliefs, and sins being passed down." In my opinion, a generational curse is an action that becomes a bloodline behavior due to unhealed trauma, lifestyle, or condition. Far too often, we as a culture have viewed healing or seeking help as a sign of weakness—thus, permitting unhealed circumstances to become a way of life.

Don't believe me? Put a checkmark next to the following statements that apply to you:

_____ A single mother raised me; thus, I am a single mother now.

_____ I was raised to think "money is the root of all evil." Because of that, I have allowed my lack of understanding of money to keep me in poverty.

_____ My father used to beat me for being emotional. Now, I am serving fifteen years to life because my emotions got the best of me.

_____ My grandmother had my mother as a teenager; thus, I am a teenage mother.

_____ My father was incarcerated, and I ended up becoming his cellmate or incarcerated myself.

_____ My family gambled, and as a result of watching them, I gamble now.

_____ I witnessed my mother get physically abused. Now I'm a victim of domestic violence.

_____ My mother was sexually assaulted as a child; I was sexually assaulted as a child; my child was sexually assaulted.

_____ I was raised in poverty, and although I know there's more to experience in the world, I can't see myself leaving the block.

_____ We were taught to "speak and function as a child." So, I raised my child to "speak and function as a child," but his naïve and gullible behavior got him killed.

_____ I witnessed my grandmother tolerate things just to keep the family together. Now I am finding myself staying in situations longer than I should.

I could go on and on, but I'm sure you get the point. How many of those did you check? Whether consciously or unconsciously, generational curses or trauma are things that are either taught or witnessed. Consider this last point—nine times out of ten, your ancestors were enslaved if you are African American. They were taken from their country, women were raped (sex slaves to bear children), men became laborers (providers), and families were sold (single parents). They witnessed abuse (became abusers), ran away for freedom (changed the narrative but kept the mindset), became free (maintained the traditions of slavery but added new concepts of survival), started families (passed on the mindset), and created new generations (passed on the mindset). And as you see, the cycle continues. The only differences between the generations are many were afforded the opportunity to go to school, others fought for freedom or human rights, a few served in the military, and the rest were incarcerated. As families grew and new traumas were added, the initial unhealed pain and struggle heightened.

Again, since therapy or seeking professional mental services are dishonored within the African American community, the trauma of the past continues to exist. However, through this book, I have vowed to help you identify it and change the narrative so you can break the chains keeping you in bondage. Moreover, I intend to help you heal through the journey by challenging you to face your truth and give life to your narrative. Healing is what unleashes the bitterness so we can become better. Becoming better! Better mindset! Better financial situation! Better love life! Better relationships with family and friends! Just being a better person who is committed to evolving. People say, "You are not your diagnosis." Well, allow me to remind you that you are not your past. You are not your mother's pain or your father's failure. You are a woman or man who might have been raised in hell, but you have the key to get to heaven here on earth.

Thank you for taking this journey of healing, acceptance, and change with me. Your breakthrough is on the way. Let's get started!

Commitment of Forgiveness

We are often too hard on ourselves. This can be reflected in the emotions we experience and the guilt, shame, and fear regarding how we feel. Writing a letter of self-forgiveness can prompt us to be more forgiving and refocus our thinking on being more accepting, caring, and supportive of ourselves and others. As we prepare to do healing work, I would like you to identify a situation where you felt your emotions were out of control or unwelcoming. Whether it was you responding to a person's behavior toward you or how you treated yourself after having a bad encounter with someone else. Before you can heal, you must forgive yourself for what you have put yourself through. As we have all come to understand, the only person who owes us anything is us. The key to becoming better is practicing self-forgiveness and trusting yourself to remain positive even when faced with adversities.

In the following space, write a brief letter to yourself expressing forgiveness and acceptance for who you are and how you seek to do better. No one needs to read it. Therefore, you are safe to be open regarding your feelings. After you have finished, read what you have written, recognizing what happened and what caused you to mishandle yourself. Then forgive yourself. The more you apologize and do better for yourself, the more people will better treat and manage you. By understanding forgiveness, you will be more successful while journaling and completing the assignments within this book.

Dear _____ (insert your name),

I'm sorry for...

_____

_____

_____

_____

_____

_____

_____

_____

_____

_____

_____

_____

_____

_____

_____

_____

_____

_____

_____

_____

_____

_____

_____

_____

_____

_____

_____

_____

_____

_____

_____

_____

_____

_____

_____

_____

_____

_____

With Love,
Myself

PART ONE:
I'M NOT BITTER

I Never Asked for This, But God Did!

How many of you knew there was a curse in your bloodline? Was learning how to survive more important than playing with toys, making friends, or learning yourself? For some, we discovered just how cruel life could be when we watched as our friends got picked up at school by their dads while we didn't even know ours. Or how about those with a mother who worked so much that her friends and the babysitters started feeling like your next of kin. How many of you remember the loud growling of your empty stomach because there wasn't enough food to eat? How many of us knew, as babies, that this was the life waiting to greet us? As much as we hated our parents or childhood, we didn't understand that the behaviors and trauma were caused by generational curses or family traditions birthed from the infamous saying, "That's how we've always done it."

Whether we agree to disagree, our parents gave us either what they could, had, or understood from their upbringing. Don't believe me? Speak with your parents, aunts, uncles, or grandparents. Ask how they were raised and the lessons they were taught. After the conversation, compare your childhood to theirs. I guarantee you that seventy-five percent of what you went through, they did, as well...if not worse. When I completed this exercise, I discovered my dad's father had been absent from his life.

Even though we get mad and blame our fathers for the bad decisions made because of their absence, is that always fair? You're probably yelling, *Yes! He could have decided to be better for his children because he should've known how it felt to be fatherless.* But let's be honest. How many times have you known better but did not do better? Not making excuses, but I still wear the scars from my father's inconsistency and blame him for my mishaps. But should I? Did my father have the tools to be the man I needed? Did your father, being fatherless, know what to do to save you from your mistakes? When it comes to my mother, she lost her mother when she was two years old. As a result, she and her brother were forced to live with family because their father decided to move on with his life. He relocated to Birmingham, Alabama, got married, and enjoyed living his new life. Not only did she lose her mother, but she also lost her father. My mother immediately went from being an innocent child to learning how to survive with feelings of pain and abandonment. The curse continues.

Before we dig deeper, have you ever considered your parents' story? Do you know what trauma they've dealt with in their life? In the space provided, write out their story and then list what tools (mental and emotional) you feel they needed to possess to be the parent you wanted them to be.

_____

_____

_____

_____

_____

_____

_____

_____

_____

_____

Dr. Katrina R. Sparks

_____

_____

_____

_____

_____

_____

_____

_____

_____

_____

_____

_____

_____

_____

_____

_____

_____

_____

How did you do? Based on their story, what tools were you able to identify that they failed to use when it came to parenting you? Were they fully equipped to be the best mommy and daddy with what they had learned? If your parents' story is like many of ours, unfortunately, learning how to survive and being a provider outweighed being loving, affectionate, and present. Let's be clear; I haven't always felt this way. My way of thinking is a result of my healing. So that you can understand how I got here, allow me to share my story.

My Story!

Life for me started in Westbury, Long Island, NY. Both my parents migrated to New York from the south, seeking better opportunities. My mother is originally from Alabama, and my father is from Georgia. My mother's best friend, Larnette Fowler's mother Ms. King, named me Katrina. They considered naming me Rena after my father's mother, but "Katrina Rena" didn't sound right. I was named Katrina Renee Sparks instead. I am my father's youngest daughter and the only surviving child of my mother.

Although my parents were married, my father's presence was inconsistent. He was a horse groomer, which required him to always be on the road. Wherever the horses, owners, and jockeys traveled, he would go. My mother, on the other hand, earned a cosmetology license, became a hairdresser, later worked as a maid for a white Jewish family and then secured a career with Amtrak. Here's a random, but heartbreaking fact — my mother knew John Lewis's father, the American politician and civil rights activist, and was visiting her father when the bombing occurred at the 16th Street Baptist Church in Birmingham. Four girls—Addie Mae Collins, Cynthia Wesley, Carole Robertson and Carol Denise McNair—were killed in that bombing in 1963.

Due to my father's inconsistent presence and my lack of relationship with his side of the family, I don't know much about him or his upbringing. But growing up, I slowly became introduced to the generational curse that has plagued both of my bloodlines— fatherless child and emotionally unavailable mother. If you read closely, you might see your story in my truth.

FATHERLESS CHILD

One of the biggest curses that plague a family, especially African Americans, is a father's absenteeism or inconsistencies. Every little girl looks forward to receiving daddy's hugs and compliments, dancing on his feet while he leads, and sitting on his lap as he reads stories to her. She longs for the daddy-daughter dance, feeling safe and protected, and for him to wipe away her tears. How many of you had your daddy pick you up from school on a regular basis? How many doctor's appointments did he go to with you? If you are reading this and your daddy was present, active, and someone you looked up to as your hero, consider yourself lucky! However, this story is for the little girls who weren't so fortunate, and because of it, they are hurt and seeking healing.

My father was present throughout my childhood. However, his in and out of my life and lack of communication made me develop anger towards him. I must admit I shared great moments with my daddy, though. I remember going to the horse track with my dad when I was a kid. For him, it was another day of work, but for me, it was our special time together. I enjoyed helping him care for and feed the horses. Then there were the times he would surprise me by being there to pick me up after school let out. Another of my fondest memories is when he would have me step on his feet, and we would dance. I must add that my dad loved music—the blues, to be exact. I loved my daddy, and he loved me.

I recall a time when he went from being my daddy to my superhero. One day, he took me to kindergarten. Me being a kid, I was running around, not paying attention, and I ran into blowing ash from a cigarette. Chile, when that ash got into my eye, I screamed blue murder. With blurry, tear-filled eyes, I looked around for my daddy and saw him running towards me. He quickly picked me up, consoled me, and immediately took me to the emergency room. Typically, in a situation like that, a child would have called out for their mommy, but for the first time, I was comfortable and at peace with only my dad being there. After they diluted my eye, everything was fine.

When people say there's nothing like a daddy and daughter bond, believe them. Although my dad broke many promises and did not show up consistently like I needed him to, it did not affect my love for him. However, when my parents called it quits, my father not only separated himself from my mother. He abandoned me, too. When I say "quits," I mean they separated; they never officially divorced. When I asked my mother what had transpired, she simply replied that my dad was a jealous man. In addition, it was rumored that my dad was unfaithful to my mother and fathered another child. Between the secrets and silence still to this day, I may never get the truth about my father's story. After leaving my mother, my dad relocated to Columbus, Georgia, where he resided until his death.

During my teenage years, my father and I were in contact off and on. I kept making plans to go and visit him, but having unhealed wounds from him leaving me, I never went. Each day I found reasons not to go, all the while not aware my father was dying of cancer. When I finally decided I wanted to see my dad, he passed, and I was left to deal with my many emotions of regret and sadness. *Did I just lose my father without making amends?* Eighteen and fatherless! How does one cope with going from having an inconsistent father to no longer having a father? As I was crying and sorting my emotions, another question popped into my mind: *Am I going to the funeral?* Before I could think logically, I started recalling all his broken promises. Then I reminded myself that he didn't come to my high school graduation, nor was he there for me when I had my first heartbreak. Those recollections caused me to be even more torn about whether I would go to pay my respects.

My father's sister and my mother talked about the arrangements, and not wanting to oversee the affairs, my mom sent her money to ensure my father had a proper homegoing. My aunt took the cash, and within two to three days, my father was buried. *WHAT! I didn't even get to say goodbye!* My last opportunity to find closure was taken away from me. New trauma? Indeed! Regardless of the type of relationship my father and I had, he was still my dad. No goodbye! When I asked my aunt why, she replied, "Oh, you know how these funeral homes are.

The minute they get the money, they are ready to go. Any delay would've cost us more money."

After my father passed, I was left with not only the scars of losing him but now reliving the pain of not having enough time with him during my eighteen years. Do you have any idea the number of mistakes I've made because I did not have his love and guidance? I truly believe if I had my dad in my life, I would not have made as many bad choices. His perception! His perspective! How to navigate! All of that would have helped me better choose and understand why men make some of the choices they do. My father was not perfect, but the lessons he could have taught may have saved me from much heartbreak, pain, rejection, abandonment, and repeating the cycle of becoming a single mother. Even though I am still healing from this trauma, I am taking my life back increasingly each day. It's been years since my father passed away, but there is still a void in my heart and a yearning to be able to run to him. Grief is a process by itself, but when you add trauma, it gets a bit messy.

What is your daddy story? Do you have daddy issues? As we start healing through the journey process, I invite you to journal your feelings. Write a letter to your father, either sharing how you feel or asking him for what you need to be better. If your father is deceased, write a letter offering your final forgiveness as a sign of peace. Until you acknowledge your pain and give it a voice, you're accepting your bondage. Although your dad may never read it, releasing it is your responsibility and the first step to healing.

In the space provided, write your letter to your dad. Be honest, raw, and uncut. Write your truth so you can save your tomorrow.

_____

_____

_____

_____

_____

_____

_____

_____

_____

_____

_____

_____

Dr. Katrina R. Sparks

How do you feel? For me, journaling is one of the ways I seek healing. Since we are on this journey together, allow me to introduce you to my methods. I've also shared the letter I wrote to my daddy. You will see that even though my letter is full of pain, I am at peace.

Dear Daddy,

Although I did not get to say goodbye, I want to say I love you, Dad. I wish we would've had more time to spend together. There are so many questions, and I'm still angry that I did not receive in the capacity that a little girl needs her daddy. I wish you would have made more of an effort to be with me. I would have been happy with weekly phone calls from you, more hugs, kisses, and walks to school, or you just pouring positivity and love into my spirit. The presents were good, but hearing "I love you" more and truly feeling it was all I wanted. Can I tell you a secret, Daddy? I would rather have had conversations with you about life and navigating this world as far as education, handling people, and how to deal with boys. Do you have any idea what the streets have taught me? It may sound mean or selfish because I don't know all that you were dealing with, but know I don't blame you. I forgive you. With your father being absent in your life, did you even know how to be present in mine? It's a generational curse that's never been broken, and as much as I tried, Daddy, my son also grew up without his dad. However, I pray my baby breaks it because the pain we all feel is one that will never fully heal. Please know that I love you, and I pray you are in a good place.

THE UNAVAILABLE MOTHER

Compared to being fatherless, being a single mother is another generational curse that plagues our community. I sometimes wonder if this curse is a traditional sin that cannot be stopped due to societal norms. What do I mean by that? If you look at gender roles, women have been traditionally known to be caregivers, nurturers, and homemakers. Her role was to be the mommy and take care of the children. Now before you check me, women—like men—have given their children away and abandoned them. I don't want you to think I am only bashing men. Women, past and present, have deserted their children and will continue to do so unfortunately. Please know this book is not to attack either gender on their parenting style but to shine light on the "why" to help the next generation heal. It is not my job to judge one's decision, but it is my intention to bring us peace to handle it all. Are we good? Okay, great! Let's get back to the story.

As stated previously, my mom lost her mother when she was two years old. My mother and her brother, who are eleven months apart, were raised by family members. My mother's father remarried and lived happily ever after until his death. When my mother's father passed away, my mother's stepmother moved in with us in New York. Such a caring woman, my mother took care of any and everything for anybody. Her "southern hospitality" was as strong as her need to be better than she was before. Being a motherless and fatherless child, she understood that hard work equated to surviving. In addition, can you imagine the things she witnessed and experienced while growing up in the south in the mid-'50s and '60s? From white supremacy to the civil rights movement, beating the odds with no assistance meant you did what you had to do. Because of her values, my mother desensitized her emotions to become a woman of pride and productivity. Don't get me wrong. I am not saying she did not love or wasn't happy, but it wasn't her priority.

Before I made my entrance into this world, my mother had two children. My brother was stillborn, and I had a sister who passed away due to a childhood illness. After losing two children, my mother reclaimed her life, met my father, and then I was born. Since my dad was unreliable, my mother buried herself in work to ensure she and I were provided for in his absence. Although I appreciate her for making sure I was well taken care of, I always longed for my mother's affection, validation, and motherly instinct as a child. While writing this, I realize I am not that different than my mom. Granted, she lost her mother, and her father left. But my father was inconsistent, and my mother was unavailable, thus causing me to be raised by the streets or learn about life from observing and reading. Do you see the pattern? Different journey but the same outcome! We did not receive everything we needed from those who were supposed to give it to us. That's the thing with generational curses; the narrative does not have to be the same, but the outcome is more often than not the same. This is why it's important for you to understand your parents' journey. Because if they have not healed from their trauma, it is highly likely it will also become yours.

With my mother consistently working, I immediately went from being in her arms to being in the care of a babysitter. Ms. Morgan was my first babysitter——a very mean and strict lady. She was demanding, ordering me around like, "Go sit there!" or glaring at me in a threatening manner as she shouted, "What did I say?" I can't remember a time she said anything nice. She couldn't care less about me. There were times when she would force me to sit and watch soap operas with her instead of letting me go outside to play with friends. You know, be a kid! Oh, and let me not forget the one time when she wanted me to eat soup, but I didn't want it. She had the audacity to get a roach and said, "If you don't eat the soup, I'm going to put this roach on you." There wasn't a caring bone in that woman's body. She was the worst babysitter ever. I swear, her only concern was getting paid.

People warned my mother about how Ms. Morgan treated me, but my mother ignored them since I didn't speak up and say anything. You're probably asking, "Why didn't you tell your mother?" So happy you asked! The plain and simple answer to your question is…I was scared. I knew my mother had to work, and I did not want to cause her to lose her job or make her choose between providing for me and protecting me. Thus, I grew stronger and tougher every day while in Ms. Morgan's care and did what I had to do to survive. But then came the day when Ms. Morgan announced she was moving and could no longer babysit me. But God! Finally, I was free of her and her evil ways! The neighbor across the hallway, who we called Grandma, agreed to watch me. I had a wonderful time when I was with her. She was very loving and allowed me to be a kid. But soon, I left Grandma and became a latchkey kid. It was time to grow up!

While evolving as a teenager, learning through observation became my way of life. I watched and observed what women did everywhere I could. No one ever sat me down to have a conversation or teach me about being a little girl, a teenager, or a grown woman. Learning womanhood from a woman isn't a part of my story. I remember getting my menstrual cycle, and instead of having a conversation explaining what it was or what I would be facing, my mother bought me Judy Blume's book, *Are You There, God? It's Me, Margaret.* Remember that book? That is how I learned about what I was going through. My mother's conversations with me about it were very simple. She would say, "Oh, you got your period? You're a woman now, so you got to be careful. Don't let the little boys touch you, or you might get pregnant." She didn't go into how many days it would last, the cramps, or why it even happened. Then I remember my friend telling me kissing can get you pregnant. Crazy, right?! But when children don't learn from their parents, this is the type of thing they hear, among other crazy stuff.

Furthermore, as my body developed, hormones were jumping, and others around me started defining what pretty was, my self-esteem took a dip. Being a dark-skinned sister oftentimes resulted in me being ignored or not considered beautiful among boys. Compliments and pep talks to help me overcome my self-esteem and confidence issues were something I would have welcomed from my mom. I can't recall the last time my mom told me, "Katrina, you are beautiful," or "You can do anything." Don't get me wrong; I understand she spent much of her time working and didn't have much time to pour into me, but her encouragement could have stopped me from thinking I had to pay attention to everyone who said something nice. After all, not everyone who spoke meant me good.

Who encouraged you? Who spoke confidence, worth, value, and love into you? When was the last time you had a conversation with the little girl who didn't know she was special? As grown women, it is imperative that we heal the little girl inside of us. What did you need to hear as a kid that you never heard?

In the following space, affirm and validate yourself. The more you affirm her, the more she will be able to heal. Then you will be on your way to wholeness!

_____

_____

_____

_____

_____

_____

DR. KATRINA R. SPARKS

How many of you understand how it feels to have an inconsistent father and an unavailable mother? If so, you already know what this recipe will create—a curse that will try to define us. But if you know me, you know I devised a plan to change the narrative. Or so I thought.

Surviving the Curse

Woooo! That was a lot to unpack! I hope I did not trigger anybody. If so, I apologize, but at the same time, I'm glad because you can only seek healing by awakening the hurt and pain that you are holding on to inside. I am happy I made you acknowledge your parents' story, and how, even though the trauma happened to you, it wasn't because of you. Now that was good! Preach, Dr. Sparks!

How many of you feel you are the reason for your pain? Raise your hand. How many of you are holding onto that rape, molestation, loneliness, abuse, abandonment, insecurity, and/or heartbreak as if you caused it? Who says the following... *"My birth caused my parents' separation or divorce." "My mother abused me because my appearance and behaviors reminded her of my dad,"* or, *"Because I was a developed little girl, that male figure felt the need to treat my body like a woman"?* How many of you blame yourself?

Now that the curse has invaded our lives, how do we survive with it?

Let's pause right here because that is a good question. How are you dealing with your curses? Are you coping by ways of self-medicating, alcoholism, yoga/exercise, journaling, or creating pain for others so they can feel yours? In the space provided, write how you are surviving through the curse.

_____

_____

_____

_____

_____

_____

_____

_____

_____

_____

_____

_____

Did you know that every day you leave the curse unhealed, it grows into a more toxic behavior? Moreover, we begin using it to justify our behaviors when we repeat them.

- *My dad left me. Did you think yours was going to stay?*
- *Your mother was an alcoholic, so it's understandable that you would become one, too.*
- *This is how I was raised; I don't know how to be anyone else.*
- *Being a single mother is hereditary. Welcome to the club!*
- *I allowed that man to abuse me because I saw my mother being abused.*
- *This is how all the men in my family act. Why should I be anything different?*

Who can relate to these statements? How many of you have been told one of these or been the one to say it? This is what surviving through the curse looks like. Between people affirming our pain and us validating the feeling, we tend to accept the trauma as normal. In turn, it causes us to go mentally to dark places——such as depression and low self-esteem—and experience insecurities, sabotaging thoughts, suicidal impulses, anxiety, or other mental health conditions. How many of you are living in these places because you are still surviving through the curse? For me, survival showed up as a lack of confidence, low self-esteem, and needing validation. The streets and boys became my teachers, and man, oh man, the lessons not only guided me but piled other people's curses and trauma onto my own. By the time I realized it, I was looking at a nine-month bid!

The Journey!

I didn't start hanging out until I was between fifteen and sixteen years old. Even though my mother was busy working, she was protective whenever she was home. "Be on the steps or in the house when the streetlights come on," she would tell me. If I were out too long, she would scream my name from the window. Talk about embarrassing! If she wasn't at home, there was no going out of the house to chill or having people come over. Being a latchkey kid, I was told to come straight home, lock the door, and eat tuna fish sandwiches. Can I just say I do not eat tuna fish sandwiches to this day, and let me tell you why. The eggs were not chopped up. I would get a piece of bread, slap the egg and tuna on it, grab something to drink to wash it all down, and that was my snack. Talk about traumatized! Who eats a whole egg in tuna sandwiches? But I digress!

By the time my mother got home after work, she was tired. Reviewing my homework was something she did only if she had the energy, but since I understood the importance of education, I made sure to keep good grades. Ensuring I was exposed, my mom paid for dance lessons—ballet and tap—and gymnastics. I also attended Barbizon for modeling and acting. My mom always researched the paper to find things for me to do. She even signed me up for free reading and math classes on Saturdays. In high school, I was a member of the All-City HS Chorus. Needless to say, I stayed busy and never bored.

Even though my mom wasn't the most affectionate or emotionally connected person, her work ethic was one of a kind. My mother put the capital "H" in Hustler because she could get it done with nothing. We were never on any form of public assistance, but I had everything I needed in regard to material possessions. She did not receive child support, nor did she get any inheritance from her family. My mother knew how to survive. Remember, she was parentless, and understanding early on that working was her only means of survival, she never slacked when it came to taking care of home. Out of all my mother's great qualities, I adopted her work ethic. I work seven days a week, and I always got something going on or am doing something to ensure my son and I are good. As I told you, observing was my means of learning.

Hip-Hop Gave Us Hope

As my schedule got busier, I didn't immediately catch on to the many epidemics invading America's urban cities. However, I did start bearing witness to how my neighborhood was changing. By this time, I was living in South Bronx, New York. If you are familiar with the South Bronx, you know it was nothing nice nor pretty. I don't know how many of you know, but in the 1970s, the houses of the South Bronx were set ablaze. Eighty percent of housing was lost to fires, and 250,000 people were displaced. Although the story of why differs based on who tells it, the South Bronx was my home despite not being the greatest area. In addition, the drug epidemic was evolving. It was nothing to see needles littering the ground when walking down the street. Heroin, methadone, and crack cocaine destroyed more families than deaths from cancer, high blood pressure, and HIV.

As the residents changed due to the fires, the culture adjusted. As a result, we found solitude in music and being a family. I remember playing stickball, handball, and a game called skully. We also loved to skate. Atlanta had nothing on us. *HA!* Atlanta may have had Cascade

Family Skating, but we had Skate Key. It was our spot where everyone was a celebrity. On skate night, we wore sweatshirts with our name on the front and our zodiac sign on the back, name plates around our necks, and door-knocker earrings. Don't judge! This fashion was considered, "fly", "fresh or "dope".

I am blessed to say I also witnessed the start of hip-hop back then. Hip-hop became the anthem of the inner cities. One of my fondest memories is sitting outside on crates and listening to men spit rhymes over beats that spoke to the environment and situations we all were living in. Who remembers Webster Avenue? This was the spot where deejays would go to plug in their equipment and jam in the park. I remember meeting Grandmaster Flash and the Furious Five, Boogie Down Productions, and listening to Afrika Bambaataa and Soul Sonic Force, Stetsasonic, The Treacherous Three, Funky Four Plus One More, Grandmaster Caz, and many others. Hip-hop was all around me. Graffiti was our written expression, and hip-hop was how we communicated. No matter what we were dealing with, we were creative enough to be heard and seen.

This is why I loved growing up in New York, especially the South Bronx. It prepared you for survival. We were not scared of anything; we knew the dangers of our city. We all lost a loved one or knew someone who lost someone to murder, drugs, or incarceration. So, no one considered themselves better than the other. We respected each other regardless of our circumstances. We learned to live through life. We never addressed it or dwelled on it; we just accepted it to be what it was. Even though some were comfortable in their life of curses and dysfunction, others, like myself, knew there was more to life and didn't settle. Plus, I had a mother who wasn't willing to lose her child to the streets. So, as the streets got rougher, I got busier, and the "village" kept my mom informed.

I attended A. Philip Randolph Campus High School, which is in Harlem. For those who don't know, A. Philip Randolph founded the first major Black labor union, the Brotherhood of Sleeping Car Porters, and was a civil rights activist. Most importantly, he was a Phi Beta Sigma Fraternity, Inc. member. Back to the topic, my high school years were when I needed my dad the most. From the sweet-talking boys to the peer pressure, this was the time when my need for guidance started. Like any young girl looking for love, I fell victim to my first relationship that eventually backfired. I was fourteen years old and a freshman; he was a senior. I was a cheerleader; he was on the basketball team. I just knew he liked me just as much as I loved him. Around this time, my Saturdays were free, so we spent time together then. Those times together led to me giving him my virginity, and once he got it, he was gone. *Daddy, where were you?* I was so mad and hurt. All this time, I thought he was my boyfriend, not realizing he was only doing what boys did. This experience made me more insecure because I blamed myself for him leaving. After that heartbreak, I felt I wasn't cute enough to keep a man. Back then, being light-skinned with long hair was the thing, but ya girl was brown skin, and that wasn't necessarily what was in. So, not only did I feel I wasn't good enough to love anyone, but I also believed I wasn't worthy of being loved.

First my father and now this guy. It made me question myself a lot. My self-esteem had bottomed out, and I was lost. After that, I shelled up and just focused on my schooling and other activities I was involved in. I graduated from high school in 1986 and soon after attended SUNY at Oswego, a state university in New York. Let me say this; if I knew then what I know now, I would have gone to a Historically Black College & University (HBCU) or the military—a HBCU to obtain the "Black culture" experience or the military because they offer the foundation, housing, benefits, and discounts. You see, going to college wasn't encouraged in my family. Granted, I saw the college experience depicted in movies and TV shows, but it wasn't a part of the life structure. However, with everyone around me going away to college, I started becoming interested in the experience, too. I had a lot of cousins who went to Tuskegee and Alabama State University. The plan was for me to go to Tuskegee, but remembering my time visiting the south, I decided it was no place I wanted to live. So, SUNY at Oswego had to work. Plus, I was going on a full scholarship. Yup, that indeed worked!

Since my mother couldn't drive, she had one of her friends drive us there. Mind you, I did not go on a college tour, nor did I visit the school before attending. So, when I stepped foot on campus, it was a culture shock. The buildings looked like houses. The area was rural; there were cows, grain, and grasslands. Oh, and I later found out there was no partying or clubs. There was a local bar, and that was it. *What the hell have I gotten myself into?*

Zeta Phi Beta Sorority

Allow me to set the record straight. Everyone thinks my introduction to The Divine Nine is because of my college experience. Wrong! For me, it goes back to my childhood. There was a lady by the name of Linda Williams who became a Zeta at Lincoln University in Pennsylvania in 1976. Affectionately, I called her my big sister. We attended the same church, Family Baptist Church. Then, my boyfriend David Hannah's mother was a member of Zeta through Shaw University during the '40s or '50s. Right before she succumbed to dementia, I went to see her. A soror of mine worked in a nursing home and was able to locate her for me. These two women were my introduction to the finer women of Zeta Phi Beta Sorority, Inc.

Then there was the high school I attended—A. Philip Randolph High School, which was named after a member of Phi Beta Sigma Fraternity, Inc. If you don't know, Phi Beta Sigma Fraternity, Inc. and Zeta Phi Beta Sorority, Inc. are the only constitutionally bound Greek letter organizations—"just so we are all very clear," as my Soror Syleena Johnson would say. The pastor and first lady of the second church we attended were also members of Zeta Phi Beta Sorority, Inc. and Phi Beta Sigma Fraternity, Inc. So, the blue and white family has always been a part of my life. For me, becoming a member of Zeta Phi Beta Sorority, Inc. was destined. Don't get me wrong; I researched and inquired about the other sororities, attended events and step shows, and had friends who were members. But Zeta was home. I couldn't see myself being anything else at that point. When I attended SUNY at Oswego, Phi Beta Sigma and Zeta Phi Beta Sorority Inc were not on campus. Phi Beta Sigma Fraternity was chartered during my freshman year. With the Sigma's being on the yard, I became a Sigma Dove during my sophomore year.

I remember being asked to join the organization, but at the time, I was going through some things while trying to figure out life and surviving through pain. So, I declined. However, in the spring of 1998, when the timing was right, I became a proud member of Zeta Phi Beta Sorority Inc. through Nu Psi Zeta in Peekskill, New York. I am a former member of Kappa Epsilon Zeta Chapter in the Bronx, New York, where I held the position of 3rd Anti-Basileus and founded the Archonette Auxiliary Club. I am currently a member of Zeta Phi Beta Sorority Inc., Gamma Alpha Sigma Zeta Chapter in Ghana, Africa.

SECOND YEAR

My sophomore year was a bit challenging, yet fun. Just as I started adjusting to college life, I began having very painful menstrual cycles that left me incapacitated. Unfortunately, my physician discovered I had fibroids. I remember skipping classes because I could not move due to the pain. As the condition worsened, my ability to attend classes and complete assignments became a daunting task, so I withdrew from school.

Back at home, I took a part-time job at Alexander's.

Who would have known I would meet my son's father there? He spotted me, and I saw him. He thought I was cute, and he wasn't half bad. So, we went together. I swear, it happened just like that. To this day, I can't explain to you why we moved so fast. We did not do any courting or dating. It was more like you, *I love you. Let's get married.* We were engaged within three months of meeting. I never fully got to know him; I knew of him. I had no clue who he was and what drama or trauma he was bringing.

He had left the military and enrolled in Borough Manhattan Community College, and I eventually went back to college. We were going to be a powerful couple. Even though things were not perfect, my desire to make it make sense made me ignore the signs and focus on the love. However, when I returned home, the man I met at Alexander's was not the man I remembered. After praying, I discovered he was addicted to crack cocaine. *He's an addict? And I'm pregnant!* The one generational curse I did not want after seeing what my mother had gone through. I absolutely did not want to carry that cross. *Dammit! Why, Katrina? How, Katrina?*

Was It Love or My Desperation of Being Loved?

Who can relate to this journey? Still dealing with the pains of your childhood but now adding more trauma to the mix. Why is it that we become everything we dislike or that caused us pain? Why do we repeat the cycle? Speaking from my experience, when you are a child who longed for love from a father and attention from a mother, you are more likely to fall victim to hurt, abuse, or trauma simply because you accept people without thoroughly getting to know them. You are more interested in filling a void than finding the right person. I can admit my relationship was downright wrong, but not having a father to warn me or a mother to check me, my heart said, "Girl, get your man."

How many of you moved fast in a relationship? I know I am not the only one out here who fell quickly and hard. Let's have another "come to Jesus" moment, because the only way we are going to break these chains is by facing them, speaking the experience, and being humble to the lesson learned.

In the space provided, write a time when you moved too fast and didn't get the outcome you desired.

Now that you have acknowledged this, I want you to identify why you felt the need to move fast. What were you lacking that led you to believe they were the missing piece of your puzzle? Were you seeking love, or were you desperate to be loved, no matter the cost?

_____

_____

_____

_____

_____

_____

_____

_____

_____

_____

_____

_____

_____

Again, I hope I did not trigger you, but to heal and get better, we must speak what we are holding within, no matter how ugly it is. Let me remind you to give yourself grace as you are going through this book and journaling. Yes, giving ourselves grace is easier said than done because we are so used to beating ourselves up, getting beat up by others for our mistakes, and/or repeating the very things we despise. But when we give ourselves grace, we permit ourselves to be human, not perfect.

Here are some tips to help you survive the curse when it eventually comes knocking at your door. Remember, whatever goes unhealed is welcomed.

- **Don't Be Perfect; Be Human** — No one is perfect. You're going to err by saying or doing the wrong thing. The goal is not to be perfect but to unapologetically be who you are. At the same time, learn from your mistakes so that your imperfections don't ruin your happiness.

- **Don't Let Wrong Define You** — It's okay to be wrong; however, don't let the guilt define you. Just because you made a bad choice doesn't mean your life is over. You just have to come up with a new strategy to get back on track.

- **Give Yourself Permission to Just Be** — Unless you have a cape and can fly, you're not a superwoman. Remember, you can't be everything to everybody and be nothing to yourself.

- **Seeking Help from a Professional** — I know it's a sin to seek help from a therapist. However, trying to carry the burden of pain, hurt, trauma, and illness by yourself is going to wreak havoc on your body and may eventually kill you. So, unless you are ready to check out of life, get professional help to release your pain.

Who's ready to acknowledge and accept the curse so you can start healing? Aren't you ready to overcome and finally be happy? As we close out this chapter, I want to challenge you to complete one more assignment. In the space provided, list the curses you have added to your life from others on top of yours.

_____

_____

_____

_____

_____

_____

_____

_____

_____

_____

_____

_____

_____

_____

_____

_____

_____

_____

_____

_____

Great job! I am so proud of you! Now, let's get to the process of owning and overcoming. Are you ready?

WHEN THE CURSE ENTERS YOUR GENERATION

How are you feeling? I know you didn't expect to be journaling and doing healing work through your trauma and curses. But, if you know me, you know I don't do anything that is not making us better. Anyone can author a book and share their story, but for me, sharing my story for your breakthrough was more important. I hope you are enjoying your experience while learning more about me. Moreover, as you continue to read, you will continue to see that we, as women, all have the same story. However, what makes us unique is how we own and overcome the curse once it enters our life. As stated in the previous chapter, not only was I dating a drug addict, but I was also having a baby by one. Not only did the curse of single motherhood enter my life, but the demons and trauma my fiancé had also come.

OWNERSHIP!

As reckless as I was, becoming pregnant by an addict was not something I asked for, hoped for, or prayed to happen, but let's be clear, I was naive about a lot of things. It didn't help that I had become accustomed to inconsistency from men. His behaviors prior to me finding out about his addiction were normal in my eyes. Again, I found myself blaming my father. If he had been present and taught me what to expect from men, I believe I would have caught the signs earlier. But then, I realized that blaming him was not the answer. If my dad had warned me, it still would have been my decision, and when someone is "in love," they don't want nobody telling them anything. Even if someone tried to warn them, would they listen? More than likely not.

LOYAL BY DEFAULT

Right before Thanksgiving, my fiancé called to let me know he was in a detox facility but about to be released. Although hurt, being the supportive fiancé, I vowed to be there for him. After explaining everything to my mother, she said, "Y'all not living together, but he can stay on the couch. We can help." So, I went and picked him up and brought him to my house. Afterwards, I started seeing a change for the better in him. We were getting back to loving each other. Shortly thereafter, I discovered I was pregnant. Excited by the news, he promised my mother he would marry me.

"I'm going to marry her," he told her. "I'm going to be an honest man."

Things were going great, but since he did not fully detox from drugs, his fight led him to recurring stays at rehabilitation centers. As his struggle with drugs continued and his disappearances became more frequent, I started owning my circumstances. However, in my ownership, I began doubting my ability to be a good mother to my child. There were times when I confessed, "I can't have this baby." I was unhealed, juggling new hurt, dealing with insecurities, and trying to better myself to change my narrative. I didn't feel mentally or emotionally ready to be someone's mother. I remember praying and seeking God's guidance because I was torn on what to do. Why was I about to embark on the same journey I witnessed my mother struggle through? What lesson did I miss, or was I focused on the wrong thing?

One day, I shared my feelings with my mother, and she poured life into me. She affirmed, "Yeah, you may be twenty-one and still pursuing your undergraduate degree, but you will get through this." As she was assuring me, she also made it clear that there would be no applying for public assistance. Being a woman of pride and hard work, she always believed a person should handle their business, not beg for it. I owned my narrative through her encouragement and affirming that I was built for this. In addition, I promised myself that I would add my own spin to it. My motherhood journey would not look like anyone else's in my family.

TJ was born prematurely, weighing three pounds and thirteen ounces. If you ever gave birth to a premature child, you already understand how my life altered after his delivery. I was consistently going back and forth to the hospital to visit him and make sure he was developing. Once he was able to come home, I enrolled in Herbert Lehman College and secured my Bachelor of Arts in African American Studies with a concentration in Early Childhood Education. With education being the key, I was committed to finishing my degree. Like Taraji P. Henson, I graduated with my baby on my hip. Not literally, but I was a mother and finally a college graduate.

After graduating, I focused on being a mother and caring for my son. No longer depending on his dad to assist, my mother and I ensured TJ was good. Besides, I couldn't locate TJ's dad half the time anyway. Soon, I started becoming bitter. My animosity towards my son's father grew because, even though I had money and was doing the best I could, I still needed my mother's help. Around this time, she should have been preparing for

68

retirement and finally living her life without the responsibility of caring for anyone other than herself. Although she did not mind, I grew angrier and angrier. I couldn't understand how he could not make his son a priority. Drugs meant more to him than getting himself together to be consistently present in his son's life. But, despite being bitter, I never kept TJ from him. My mother would remind me that he was TJ's father, and whenever he came with something, she would say, "That *is* his son. Let him see him."

Listening to my mom, TJ and I would take the train to the rehab facility to spend time with his dad. During one of our visits, I got a picture of TJ with his dad. That is one of the only pictures I have of them together. As we continued to visit, I assumed he would focus on healing so he could become the father his son needed, but I was wrong. The cycle repeated, and his coming and going in and out of our lives became a distraction after a while. I wanted out!

One day, unexpectedly, he called me, sharing that he had been released from rehab and was looking to either get a job or go back into the military. Then he asked, "Well, are we going to get back together?" *The nerve!* I replied, "No, I just need you to do right by your son." With all of the back and forth and his broken promises, I no longer wanted to be bothered. Of course, my response was not what he wanted to hear, and he went missing in action again. I could not get in touch with him at all. I later found out he met someone else, had two kids, and married her. Doesn't this story sound all too familiar?

Why do men leave the first family and go create a new family and offer them everything you were asking for? Was it that I was not catering to the inconsistencies or that I was not partaking in his demons? Although I broke it off, how could he get it right for them and not us? I found myself asking the same questions my mother and uncle asked about their dad and that I was asking about my dad. A vicious cycle that never stops. It just gets perfected as new generations become more creative, but, Lord, we have to do better.

As people found out about what I was going through, I finally learned the story of my baby's father. Come to find out, there were a lot of dysfunctions in his family. He, like myself, was a fatherless child. His mother was very spiritual, but she did not like me. They constantly questioned the legitimacy of TJ being related to them. You see, my son is dark-skinned, and they are light-skinned. However, TJ's mother is dark-skinned, and so is my family. But, for giggles, I agreed to a paternity test. Already knowing the results, I went along with the dysfunction. Afterwards, when everyone had the results, I put on my cap of confidence and became the best mother I could be. I gave myself permission to evolve as a woman.

EMBRACING MY NEW NORMAL, SINGLE MOTHERHOOD

Katrina Renee Sparks, you are a single mother! Having owned my decision and accepted my choice of leaving his father, I became proactive and handled business. Now don't be fooled! Even with my proactiveness and positive attitude, there were times when I was stressed beyond belief. While trying to maintain motherhood, pursue my master's degree, and hold down a job, there were days I dreaded getting out of bed. Now understanding my mother's exhaustion, I still got up and showed up. My life was no longer about me; it was about my son and me becoming a significant role model for him.

When I wasn't in school or working, I spent time with TJ. We would go to the children's museum and the zoo, and he took swimming lessons. Once I had a little extra cash, he and I took trips to Puerto Rico, the Bahamas, and many other places. The more I took ownership, the more I stopped focusing on how this detour affected my life. Instead, I gave thanks for how this detour permitted me to be able to share my love with someone who actually appreciated it. I converted my embarrassment into a plan that made being a single mother manageable. I knew dropping out of school wasn't an option! I knew becoming a welfare statistic wasn't an option! So, while pregnant, I came up with a plan. I wrote it down and followed my own advice. Moreover, I gathered my village, reassuring their support so I knew who I could depend on and who I could not. How were they going to step in and help? Who would babysit while I was in school or whenever I had to get something done? Things got a lot easier when my mother retired because she had more time to help me if I needed her.

Now, if you are thinking, *I don't have a village. I don't have people I can turn to because everybody's busy*, then you're going to have to come up with a plan B and C. Start looking into childcare and any other programs that offer babysitting. And if your funds are low, there are programs for single mothers. Always remember, just because you are alone, it doesn't mean you have to do it alone.

As you see, the more I owned my circumstances, the more at peace I became with my story. I did not mistreat my son because his dad was a deadbeat. I did not beat myself up because I carried the curse into my life. Instead, I accepted my role and stood in my position.

What do you need to take ownership of? When you start taking accountability and stop blaming others for your journey, you take back your life and peace. In the space provided, write out what you need to take back. Yes, that man may have left you, but he wasn't good for you anyway. Yes, he abandoned you, but where would you be if he had stayed? The day I converted my anger to "thank yous" was the day I felt free. Are you ready to be free? Always remember, whoever owns your heart, controls your life.

_____

_____

_____

_____

_____

_____

_____

_____

_____

_____

_____

_____

_____

DR. KATRINA R. SPARKS

Finally embracing my new life, it was time to get to work and create a good life for my son and me. One day, a lady at church who sat on the board asked if I wanted a job, knowing that my background was in education and speech pathology. I agreed and landed a job as a special education teacher working at a school right down the street from where we lived. Working there gave me good training. It also taught me that every staff member is not collaborating with you; some are actually working against you. So now, on top of working and maintaining, I had to concern myself with watching my back.

As I tried to deal with everything, I received a call that would change my life. "Ms. Sparks, your son has been diagnosed with autism," the caller said. At the time, TJ was four years old. Having worked with special education children, I had an inkling something was wrong, but being in denial, I did not want to address it. However, now with a diagnosis, I started questioning myself. What did I do? Did the drugs in his father's system cause it? Then I started hearing that too much mercury could cause it. This news gave me more reason to panic because I ate fish while pregnant. All sorts of things started going through my mind, and as I was focused on me, I had to stop and ask myself, *What are you going to do for your son? Your son is an African American boy in a system that is not concerned with helping him but instead labeling him.* Instantly, I took the focus off me and fell to my knees to pray. *God, give me the strength to help me save my son.*

When It Rains, It Pours!

Because TJ was born prematurely and presented as a NICU baby, we were always at doctor's appointments. For some reason, the soft spot in the middle of his head was not closing timely. To figure out why they kept performing radiology scans to determine the cause. After numerous visits and no answers, I decided to change doctors and take him to an African physician who was committed to finding answers. He managed to get my son evaluated through the Committee of Preschool Special Education (CPSE). As TJ was being evaluated, they discovered he wasn't talking much and wouldn't always make eye contact. When he did say something, he would always repeat it. In addition, he had a lot of energy—always running all over the place, a very hyper child. At three years old, they diagnosed him with a condition called Communication Delay Disorder. According to Stanford Medicine, [1]"A child with a communication disorder has trouble communicating

---

[1] Communication Disorders in Children (stanfordchildrens.org)

with others. He or she may not understand or make the sounds of speech. The child may also struggle with word choice, word order, or sentence structure. There are several types of these disorders. They are:

- **Mixed receptive-expressive language disorder** — A child has developmental delays and problems understanding spoken language and speaking.
- **Expressive language disorder** — A child has developmental delays and problems speaking.
- **Speech-sound disorders** — A child has a tough time expressing words clearly past a certain age.
- **Childhood-onset fluency disorder** — This is also known as stuttering. It starts in childhood and can last throughout life.
- **Social communication disorder** — A child has trouble with verbal and nonverbal communication that is not caused by thinking problems."

I accepted this diagnosis and was dedicated to doing whatever it took to help my son. However, new behaviors started appearing just when they thought they had the answer. While attending a special education school, they officially diagnosed him with autism. Not knowing about autism, I never related TJ's condition to that. When I thought of autism, I associated it with non-verbal children who ticked back and forth, flanked their hands and engaged in echolalia to self-stimulate themselves. Understanding that my son's condition needed me to love him in a unique way, I became engrossed in learning more about it. As I researched, I learned that [2]"Autism, or autism spectrum disorder (ASD), refers to a broad range of conditions characterized by challenges with social skills, repetitive behaviors, speech and nonverbal communication. Signs of autism usually appear by age 2 or 3. Some associated development delays can appear even earlier, and often, it can be diagnosed as early as 18 months." As I continued reading and researching, I learned that [3]"Children and adults with autism have difficulty with verbal and non-verbal communication. For example, they may not understand or appropriately use:

- Spoken language (around a third of people with autism are nonverbal)
- Gestures
- Eye contact
- Facial expressions
- Tone of voice
- Expressions not meant to be taken literally"

---

[2] What Is Autism? | Autism Speaks
[3] What Are the Symptoms of Autism? | Autism Speaks

MY SON'S DIAGNOSIS IS NOT MY PUNISHMENT

Okay, Katrina, not only are you a single mother, but you also have a son on the spectrum. No longer concerned with how it was caused, I focused my attention on what help he needed. I must admit, with this condition not being wildly acknowledged or understood, I felt alone—like no one understood me. In addition, I grew fearful, embarrassed, and protective. Don't get me wrong; I never regretted or felt ashamed for having my son. But when people don't understand, and you have to explain, it tends to lead to judgment. Therefore, to protect him and save others from my attitude, I would not bring him around when I was invited to events or parties. After a while, explaining his condition became daunting.

My mother, on the other hand, didn't understand the diagnosis and thought it was just a phase. She would always say, "He's going to snap out of it. He'll get it together. I'm going to go to church and pray to Jesus. God's going to make it all right. TJ will snap out of it and be normal again." How could I come to grips with my son's diagnosis with her preaching from a place of denial? I understand the old-school "give it to God" mentality, but I honestly didn't want to hear it. She kept saying it over and over again until, one day, I snapped. "He is normal!" I told her. "There's nothing wrong with him. This is the way God made him. Either you're going to help, or I'm going to go out on my own and do what I need to do." Although I knew she meant no harm and wanted to be positive, it became too overwhelming for me.

As I learned more and became familiar with his behaviors, I dropped the mommy guilt and accepted our reality. TJ started coming around, and I started including him in everything I did. He even hung with me around my fraternity brothers and sisters. Hiding him was no longer an option. As he grew up, I continued educating myself and speaking to sorors and brothers in the field about things I needed to know. I didn't want anybody to sugarcoat anything, as I wanted to understand. But then, one Sunday, while at church, my protection for my son was tested, and after my response, no one ever again tried me about my son's diagnosis.

While in church, TJ was making noise, and in the middle of the service, the pastor said, "Could someone help the parent with the child?" Oh, my goodness! I was so embarrassed! I grabbed TJ, walked him outside, and started crying. Adding insult to injury, some woman came over to me and said, "Oh, he's okay. He's not crazy." With much built-up rage, I replied, "Nobody said he was crazy! This is my son! Anything else?" She quickly walked away. She learned that day never to come for mine. I am a single mother! I am a mother of a child with autism, and I am okay with that!

As time marched on, I enrolled in the Masters in Special Education at Long Island University in Brooklyn. Also, I worked for the Board of Education in New York City. Through my employer, there was a program where they offered partial scholarships. After securing that, I paid the balance by cashing in all of my savings' bonds I had received since birth and from the money I had saved from working every weekend—Saturday and Sundays from nine o'clock until five or six o'clock. With my mother's help, I not only graduated with my Master's within a year and a half, but I graduated with no debt. After that, I went back and earned a second Master's degree in School Administration and Supervision from Massachusetts College of Liberal Arts at North Adams, MA., a Master's from Argosy University in Educational Specialist/Educational Leadership, and a Doctorate of Philosophy in Professional Studies in Education from Capella University.

As you can see, I changed my entire narrative. I went from battling the ills of generational curses to signing my name as Dr. Katrina R. Sparks. As I said before, I may not have received all I needed from my parents, but I became everything I needed to be for myself and my son. Plus, I educated myself so that I am aware no matter what stage or age of life I am in.

I DEMANDED RESPECT

Finally embracing my new journey, I felt a change of scenery would give me a new perspective. So, I secured a job in Yonkers (Westchester County). Unlike the five boroughs, Yonkers is different. There are nice parts and then you turn the corner and are like, "what did I just walk into"?

The school district had recently hired a superintendent from Texas whose primary purpose was to break up the union. As he tried to perform that assignment, he saw a bigger problem—there were not enough teachers representing the children sitting in the classroom. Thus, his mission changed. From 1998 to 1999, he hired a team of Black and brown teachers and staff. The school already had two Black teachers but needed more.

As the minorities came, leadership was bothered by the fact that the superintendent was not hiring more Irish and Italians. They did not accept the fact that schools were now desegregated. With kids moving all over due to the integration law, children were no longer confined to the neighborhood school. Leadership wanted the Irish to stay with the Irish and the Italians to stay with the Italians. However, the Black and Latinos had to stay on their side. I remember a former Italian principal had a problem calling me Dr. Sparks. He could not come to say Dr. Sparks, and if he did not address me correctly, I ignored him. He once said, "If you don't answer, it is considered insubordination." As a response, I went straight to the union and told them to tell him that I said, "I consider it discrimination that he doesn't address me by name, but he addresses everyone else who has their doctorate that doesn't look like me." I also remember going at it with an assistant principal who had another Black lady go after me. Why?! It seemed like the more I elevated, the more demons I had to fight to demand respect. No matter how people saw me or what preconceived notations they had, I worked hard, earned everything I had, and had the right to be respected for it. I paid the price to be the boss, and I will protect it at all costs.

PART TWO:
I'M BETTER

HEALING THROUGH THE JOURNEY

Healing, for me, was when I traveled to Africa. It was something about the energy, vibration, and sense of home that made me do a lot of self-reflecting and journaling. And if you know anything about Africa, then you know they believe in God and Jesus. It was there I met and communicated with a spiritual advisor. Not knowing me from Adam, he spoke like we grew up together. After my experience there, I connected with another spiritual advisor as soon as I returned home. She understood everything I was talking about without me having to tell her what had happened. Immediately following, seeking spiritual guidance became a part of my healing process. In addition, I took their advice and started doing more for myself. When I need a break, I will go away for three or four days to recenter, or I'll get massages. What does healing look like for you? Have you even embarked on your journey?

Before we dive further into my healing methods, I would love to help you get aligned with your desire to heal. Being clear on what you no longer want allows me to help you get clear on what you desire in life. Healing is not just about talking and releasing; it is also about realigning and rediscovering your life after going through it. The key to overcoming is being aware and clear of the goal.

In the space provided, answer the following questions. You may not know how to answer or believe you are worthy of what you are writing. But trust me, the more you write it out while creating a plan, the faster you will receive it.

Remember, manifestation happens when you believe and live as if you already have what you desire. So, put your request out there and start healing. I promise you the journey is easier that way.

Does anything from my past still affect me? What can I do to let go of my past?

_____

_____

_____

_____

_____

_____

_____

_____

Am I really who I am, or do the circumstances make me this way?

_____

_____

_____

_____

_____

Am I living my dream life? If not, what is stopping me from living my dream life?

_____

_____

_____

_____

_____

_____

What is my definition of success?

_____

_____

_____

_____

_____

_____

_____

Does not being able to live my dream life affect my mental health? If yes, explain.

_____

_____

_____

_____

_____

_____

_____

_____

_____

Answering these self-awareness questions will help you understand yourself better and help you quickly identify where you are lacking and where you need to take action. They can also help you find gratitude for your journey and pinpoint how successful you are indeed. If you are like me and love to write, I challenge you to start a journal to monitor your daily thoughts. If daily journaling seems a bit overwhelming, do it weekly. But for the sake of healing, do it.

OVERCOMING!

For me, journaling and traveling have helped me change my perspective, maintain positive self-thoughts, and encouraged me to celebrate all wins. And whenever I am down and can't seem to get it together, I seek professional help. Therapy is not a sin and does not mean you are crazy. Trust me, having an unbiased individual to hear you without judgment is God-sent. As I go into detail about the abovementioned methods, keep in mind that all of them may not work for you, but as you start your healing to overcome, at least pick one to do.

JOURNALING

Journaling has not only helped me with expressing my thoughts and feelings in writing, but it also provided a safe space for me to release. In addition, by regularly recording my thoughts, I gained insight into my feelings, behaviors, and moods. Moreover, writing has helped me process my past and prove just how far I've come. Reading back through the pages helps me reflect on where I used to be and where I am now in my life. If this is your first time journaling, allow me to offer you some steps to get started.

- **Maintain a log of successes.** Begin by writing the big ones you remember, then regularly jot down small victories that occur during the week. As you pay attention, your list will grow and inspire you.
- **Develop your intuition.** Write down questions or concerns, then take a deep breath and listen for a response from your Higher Self.
- **Cultivate an attitude of gratitude by maintaining a daily list of things you appreciate.** When you feel down, you can read through it for a boost of happiness.
- **Start writing about where you are in your life at this moment.** Describe your living situation, your work, and your relationships. Are you where you want to be?
- **For five to ten minutes, start writing in a "stream of consciousness."** Don't edit your thoughts or feelings, and don't correct your grammar. Don't censor your thoughts.

TRAVEL BECAME MY LIFE

When I wasn't working and my son was not in school, we traveled. TJ has been traveling since he was five months old. Traveling, for me, started as a little girl. With my mom working for Amtrak, I could ride the train for free. Out of all the states my mother and I could have visited, we went to Alabama every year. We went there so much that I just stopped going. Curious about seeing the world, I set my sights on international destinations. Passport stamps! Here I come!

For me, traveling is essential. Sometimes I am in awe of how we, as a culture, do not embrace travel. We will buy expensive luxury items to look good and impress people but not purchase a flight to broaden our knowledge about other cultures, foods, or traditions. How many kids do you know who never traveled or, better yet, never left their neighborhood? My son was challenged at school when a teacher did not believe he traveled. One day, my son shared with his class that he had gone to Puerto Rico, and his Caucasian teacher replied, "Oh, thank you for telling a good story today." My son really went to Puerto Rico, but because teachers don't hear about these adventures from our children, it's hard for them to believe. The last trip my son and I went on together internationally was to Dubai in 2016. When we went to Dubai, we abided by the rules, of course. I only had to cover up when I went into the Mosque.

I've been everywhere. I've visited El Salvador, Kenya, Mexico, Ghana, Togo, Colombia, Italy, Ireland, France, Iceland, Bali, Thailand, Germany, Singapore, England, Dubai, Germany, Singapore, Dominican Republic and

Amsterdam, to name a few. By the time you get this book, I am sure I will have visited more locations. I used to travel with groups in the past, but since I move differently, I travel solo. One time, I went on a trip with a group of people, and one of the girls hardly had any money. That became an issue. I know how I move, and I like to move how I like to move. One person not having money means we can't move as a group, or we have to chip in so that one person can move with us. Never again. When I share with people that I travel alone, they immediately say, "You're not scared?" I always reply, "No. I have a friend that works with Secret Service. I give my travel and lodging plans to him, my mother, and my friends, and I always post on social media. In addition, I register all of my international trips with, "The Smart Traveler Enrollment Program". The Smart Traveler Enrollment Program (STEP) is a free service that allows U.S. citizens to enroll their trip(s) with the nearest U.S. Embassy or Consulate. So, I am fine.

When posting on social media, I never put my actual location, per se. I'll just post a picture of the scenery. But, to be honest, I feel safer in some of these countries than I do living in America. It can be two o'clock in the morning, and someone will ask, "Sister, are you alright?" People in other countries are genuinely concerned about you. People are just having fun and surviving the best way they can. At this point, I am aware of what I can and cannot do. I'm not going to go down a dark alley. I know how to carry my bag. I know where not to pull out my money. The same things I do to survive in the Bronx work while traveling.

When it comes to traveling, I beg you to stop listening to what other people say. Do your research and go see the world. As I heal through my journey, traveling has helped me therapeutically. In addition to traveling, journaling has allowed me to give my feelings, emotions, and experiences a voice. It allows me to pen my experiences and keep track of my memories.

Out of all the countries, islands, and states I have visited, Africa is where I've found the most healing. Africa was always a place I wanted to visit. It was important for me to become one with who I am and where I am from. Last year, I completed the process of learning about my nationality and ethnicity through www.africanancestry.com. The process was affordable and painless. Once I received my results, I learned that my mother's side of the family is Somali, and I am from Kenya. Locating my ancestor's home was necessary because I get tired of folks believing that all Black people are from "down south." Or people say, "I'm from Africa," but then I reply, "Where in Africa? Africa is a huge continent. There's Mozambique, Zimbabwe, Niger,

Nigeria, and Benin. Where are you from?" Do you have any idea how many of us can't answer that question?

My story with Africa changed when I decided I needed a change. I was previously a part of the Zeta chapter in the Bronx. Not agreeing with the direction of the chapter, I decided to become a graduate member-at-large. Then, one day, a very good friend of mine, Anthony, who also was the president of the Ghana Sigma Chapter, advised that a Zeta chapter was being chartered in Ghana. Since there was a soror from the States who now lived in Ghana, the rest is history. After chartering, I became the first transfer member into the chapter. Now with my connection to Ghana and having sorors there, my journey of Africa has just started.

THERAPY, STOP TRYING TO BE STRONG ALONE

I know I may catch some flak for this one, but at this point in my life, I truly don't care. When you look at our culture and the rise in mental health, we all need some form of help. I get it—our ancestors and elders encouraged us to "give all our problems to the Lord." We carried the burden until God released it from us. Don't misunderstand me; I am a woman of faith who believes in Jesus. But as a walking human who gets tired and exhausted from the pain, I am okay with saying I need help here on Earth. Therapy is another form of healing for you and your child that will help you deal with things.

Do you know how many people die a day from suicide? According to the American Foundation for Suicide Prevention[4] ,"On average, there are 130 suicides per day." Would I be crazy to believe that if those same 130 people were supported by going to therapy, they would still be here? But because of the stigma around it, people are more likely to harm themselves or others rather than get help. When it comes to healing, you must understand that the power of letting go is in your willingness to communicate, whether written or verbally.

I understand families want to keep their secrets and business in-house, but someone sharing their experience to better their mental and emotional health is not snitching. It's healing. Every day that we hold and suppress things that we are struggling with, we are unconsciously reacting in a way that is toxic and/or dysfunctional. If you are serious about overcoming and healing through your pain, I challenge you to consider going to counseling and getting the help needed to help you navigate through everything. I am not just encouraging

---

[4] Suicide statistics | AFSP

this because of what I have heard but because I've gone to therapy. My son and I have gone to therapy. When you are committed to breaking generational curses, you know you can't do it alone.

Heal Through Self-Care

Taking diligent care of yourself is paramount to the success of your recovery process. People going through the healing process find that their physical, spiritual, and emotional health are all connected, and supporting one supports the others. Taking care of all aspects of yourself will increase the likelihood that you will stay well. For me, self-care is not just about caring for your inner being. It is also about taking care of your outer appearance. I'm sure you have heard the phrase, "When you look good, you feel good." Self-care is the care of your overall self because, ultimately, if you're not good, you're good for no one else. An effective self-care routine has been shown to have several important health benefits. Some of these include:

- Reducing anxiety and depression
- Reducing stress and improving resilience
- Improving happiness
- Increasing energy
- Reducing burnout
- Stronger interpersonal relationships

Before I offer you some self-care techniques, I would like you to assess your self-care. Again, being aware of your life and how you maneuver through it will help you identify what works, what needs to be incorporated, and what needs to be removed. When it comes to self-care, ask yourself the following questions:

- Is your diet fueling your body well?

- Are you taking charge of your health?

- What are you doing to nurture your relationships with family and friends?

- Are you making enough time for activities that mentally stimulate you?

- Are you doing proactive things to help you stay mentally healthy?

- What questions do you ask yourself about your life and experience?

- Are you engaging in spiritual practices that you find fulfilling?

- Do you have healthy ways to process your emotions?

- Do you incorporate activities into your life that help you feel recharged?

As you can see, self-care is more than relaxation, manicures, pedicures, or massages. This part of the process requires you to strategize a plan you will commit to. An effective self-care plan should be tailored to your life and your needs. It needs to be something created by you, for you. Customizing your self-care plan can be a preventative measure to ensure you don't get overwhelmed, overstressed, or burned out. As you are building your self-care plan, the following steps can be helpful:

- **Know your stressors:** Think about what causes stress and consider ways you might address stress before it affects you.

- **Be prepared for the detours:** Give yourself grace when you don't get it right the first time. The more you understand that "things just happen" in your healing journey, the more you will be prepared for the detours.

- **Celebrate small wins:** You don't have to tackle everything all at once. Identify one small step you can take to begin caring for yourself better.

- **Pencil in time for yourself on your calendar:** Make self-care a priority even when you don't feel like it. When caring for all aspects of yourself, you'll find that you can operate more effectively and efficiently.

7 Elements of Self-Care

As stated above, self-care isn't just about finding ways to relax. It's about taking care of yourself mentally, physically, emotionally, financially, spiritually, and socially. In order to care for your health and well-being, it is important to find a balance that allows you to address each of these areas. Sometimes you may need more self-care in one specific area to restore balance or find relief from a stressor in your life.

Mental Health

Protecting and maintaining positive mental health is imperative to your overall well-being. From thinking to what you download in your mind influences your psychological well-being and decision-making abilities. Mental self-care also includes doing things that keep your mind sharp so you can process things as they occur. I understand that mental health care is a personal journey because it also connects our emotional state, personality traits, and attitude demeanor. However, I would still like to offer some suggestions of the things I do to keep me sharp and "on-point" as I do the work in my fifties.

- **Disconnect from Electronics.** For me, I cut off all electronic devices before going to bed. Unbelievably, being so accessible can rob you of time to reflect and relax. Whatever the world needs from you can wait until the morning.
- **Giving Gratitude.** Knowing your journey and recognizing just how far you've come helps you become grateful for the opportunity to have another chance. I am always giving honor and thanks to God for allowing me the ability to put my feet on the floor in the morning.

- **Meditate.** In the morning, I listen to an app called Abide Meditation[5]. This app offers you meditation by using the bible. The meditation is about two minutes. A person speaks in a nice model tone while either teaching or affirming God's promise.
- **Pace with Patience.** Learning to be present and at peace requires you to move with patience. I never understood why people live their lives in such a rush. I get it, we may oversleep or lose track of time, but if you understood the amount of stress and tension you add to your mind and body when you rush around, you would stop. Life is stressful enough. Stop adding to it and simply slow down.

Physical Health

Taking care of your body and its organs will help it run efficiently. Physical self-care includes how you fuel your body, how much sleep you're getting, how much physical activity you are doing, attending healthcare appointments, and taking medication as prescribed. As you can see, it is more than just maintaining your gym membership and massage appointments. In my opinion, physical self-care is the most critical area because if your temple is not right, you can't function.

---

[5] Home – Abide

- **Exercise.** It's the Peloton for me. And a side note, if you use the Peloton, you have to work out with Alex Toussaint, a Peloton instructor. He's a beast and gets me going. The most important thing is to do some form of exercise (cardio, strength, or a combination of both) at least 3-4 days a week.
- **Maintaining Health Appointments.** As much as I don't like medical appointments or being poked, I make sure I go to the doctor. Plus, I have insurance, and since it's not cheap, I utilize it for everything. Remember to get your annual mammograms, and if you are at the age recommended for a colonoscopy, be sure to get that done, too. Prevention is key to a long life.

Emotional Health

According to Tri-State Memorial Hospital[6], emotional self-care is "to become aware of, and identify, what you are feeling, and then allow yourself to lean into the feelings in a way that honors yourself and your emotions. We can try to ignore, deny, and suppress our emotions, but eventually they come out, one way or another. Take time to acknowledge and express your

---

[6] The Importance of Self-Care - Tri-State Memorial Hospital (tristatehospital.org)

feelings: sadness, fear, frustration, overwhelmed, anger; be curious and accepting of them, without being judgmental." This element is also important because it's us controlling our feelings. The day we get our emotions intact will be the day our lives will forever change.

How many of you are dealing with a situation because your response caused friction? Our emotions can cause us to step outside of character to respond in a way that adds stress rather than resolving it. I know you may be saying, *Katrina, I hear what you are saying, but people can't treat me any kind of way,* and I get that. But you don't have to reply recklessly. Finding the right balance is key, and silence works just as good.

- **Do they even know you are mad?** Throughout my life, I have learned that when you get upset, cry, and throw tantrums while trying to get your point across, you are doing more damage to yourself, not them. To be completely honest, that person does not care about your reaction. Sure, you have the right to break glasses and yell at the top of your lungs, but the situation you are reacting to is ignoring you. So, save your energy and find another way to express yourself.
- **Think before you speak**. I've learned to assess situations and analyze everything before I react.

For example, have you ever been driving and somebody cuts you off? Your first reaction is probably to curse, yell, honk your horn, etc. For me, I let them go and remain calm. Apparently, they are rushing and have somewhere to be. Now, not to say I do not, but what people don't get to do is destroy my day by their choice. As long as there is no accident and they don't hit me, I pray for them to reach their destination safely.

- **Silence is a conversation**. Please know that you don't have to speak every time you are spoken to. You know how we hate receiving "silent treatment" in relationships. Well, chile, silence is louder than speaking, and it protects your peace by not adding energy to a situation. If saying no is a complete sentence, then silence is the cherry on top.

Financial Health

Financial health is the extent to which individuals can comfortably meet their financial needs and commitments now and in the future. A number of factors impact one's financial health into the future, including their amount of savings, borrowing behaviors, retirement investments, and how much of their income is being allocated to fixed expenses. Measuring financial health relies on six indicators, two in each of the following three categories:

Spend
- Spend less than income
- Pay bills on time

Save
- Have sufficient liquid savings
- Have sufficient long-term savings

Borrow
- Have manageable debt
- Maintaining a good credit score

I have always been a saver and a hustler. I love money. I love making money. I love for my money to create experiences for me. I love to watch my money make money through saving and investing. A good financial lifestyle is essential to your overall mental, emotional, and physical health. Have you ever completed your budget for the month and noticed you had more bills than income? How did that make you feel? How high did your stress levels reach? Having money and knowing how to keep it helps keep your stress levels down. Here are some strategies for maintaining a healthy financial life:

- **You need multiple streams of income.** As much as I want to believe the old mindset around money, it's hard to see my lifestyle in the midst of struggle. Between recessions and inflation, it is imperative that everyone has more than one source of income. Whether a side hustle or having a garage sale, earning more money will help you as the cost of living rises.
- **Investing is your friend.** Everyone does not understand investing, but between this and real estate, it is how individuals generate wealth.
- **Invest in insurance policies.** Too many of us are leaving this earth without proper estate plans. When it comes to insurance policies, or as some may call them, "just in case" plans, they are needed to protect your children and/or family after you transition. And this is not just about life insurance. Make sure you have homeowners, rental, medical, auto, and business insurance to ensure you are protected and have the coverage to seek help and assistance should something arise.
- **Shop on a budget.** I always look for a bargain. I don't think you should ever have to pay full price. Everything is negotiable. I'm not saying you shouldn't buy what you want, but please spend wisely.

- **Diversify your portfolio.** As stated above, having multiple income streams is essential to your overall financial health. Here are eight types of income you should consider:

  o **Earned Income.** Money earned in exchange for work.

  o **Profit Income.** When you sell products for a higher rate than they initially cost you.

  o **Interest Income.** Money earned by loaning money and charging interest or from a deposit or savings account.

  o **Residual Income.** When a product you have created continues to produce money for you.

  o **Rental Income.** Money earned by renting out a property or asset.

  o **Royalty Income.** Money earned from leasing or loaning a product, idea, or concept that you own to someone else.

  o **Dividend Income.** Money earned from publicly-invested companies for purchasing a share of it.

  o **Capital Gains.** An act of investing in a product or possession for a lower price with the motive of selling it for a higher cost.

Spirituality

Growing up, we were taught religion, religion, religion, and more religion. *God is everything! Jesus is everything! If you don't do this, you're going to hell...you're going to hell...you're going to hell. Get your life, and get right with God,* was all I heard. Now, before you give me the side eye, I am not suggesting that it is not important to seek a church home or spiritual guidance to guide you through life. I encourage everyone to connect to a higher power in order to maintain your faith, sanity, and fullness. Cause, trust me, journeying through life alone is not mentality safe. As for me, as I got older, I turned off religion and became anew spiritually. What is the difference, you may ask? Christianity.com[7] explains the difference as, "Spirituality is personal; religion is institutional." When it comes to religious participation[8], it is said to involve "collective and individual "prayer, meditation;" "worship, moral conduct, right belief, and participation in religious institutions." In contrast, spirituality is "non-religious experiences, which help a person get in touch with their spiritual selves through quiet reflection, time in nature, private prayer, yoga, or

---

[7] What Is the Difference Between Religion and Spirituality? (christianity.com)
[8] What Is the Difference Between Religion and Spirituality? (christianity.com)

meditation." For me, focusing on my connection with God is more important than going to church and following a person or congregation. I am not persuading you or trying to change your mindset on your spiritual walk. This is merely my life. However, I do encourage you to incorporate faith in your journey. Who you are necessarily seeking "help" from is up to you.

Social Health

Over the years, we always thought quantity was always good. In this season of my life, I'm looking for quality. I can count on one hand how many good friends I have in my life. When it comes to my social life, whether relationships or friendships, it's all about respect, loyalty, honesty, and genuinely caring. Communicating daily is not required as we are all active and living life, but knowing that if I call in need and you are there is what matters to me. We can do check-ins, send a text, or even Facetime. Hearing your voice or seeing you is all I need to ensure you are truly good. Because I know sometimes, we say everything is okay, but it is not.

In addition, maintaining a good social life requires you to review how you interact with others. Social wellness is more vital to our overall health than one may realize. Who you spend time with or talk to can indirectly or directly impact who you become. Influence is addictive! Here are three tips when it comes to making and analyzing your social life:

- **Set Boundaries.** Setting boundaries is a way to honor yourself and your needs, values, and limitations. It's a way to show that you're looking out for yourself and taking your well-being seriously. Stressful, unsatisfactory relationships can cause your mental health to take a hit, so maintaining boundaries is a great preventative measure.

- **Respect and Love Yourself.** One of the most common misconceptions about self-care is that it's a form of selfishness. It's quite the opposite! When you love and respect yourself, your mood becomes more positive, you become more confident, and you're more likely to socialize with good intentions.

- **Create a Safe Support System.** When we face adversity, it's essential to have someone to lean on. Far too often, we allow life's difficulties to dwell within us because we are "strong." Not only can this affect your physical well-being, but it also can drive us to create mental health issues such as anxiety, depression, post-traumatic stress disorder, suicidal thoughts, etc. When you seek help, it allows you to make a connection and receive the strength needed to overcome the story.

Affirming Yourself Through Healing

Affirm Yourself

As we've grown and matured, my mother affirms me now! Sometimes I can have on an outfit, and she'll say, "Oh, that's a pretty outfit, Katrina," and I'll respond, "Thank you." At times, I'm nonchalant about it because I feel she's trying to make up for the times she didn't do it. Even though affirming was one of the things I needed more of from my mom, I have come to realize that her lack of affirming was not intentional. As we have discussed, my mother lost her mother at a very young age, and I can assure you that she was never affirmed, especially being a dark-skinned woman in the south. I'm sure no one took the time to compliment her or boost her self-esteem. Moreover, I can almost guarantee she was ridiculed or disrespected by

Caucasians in school and her neighborhood. So how could I expect her to give me what she never received? I have broken that curse by affirming and acknowledging my son every chance I get. In addition, working with children, I make it my mission to affirm our youth. If I see a little girl, especially a Black or brown girl, struggling with her self-esteem, I'll greet her with a "Hello, pretty girl" or "Hey, cutie patootie." I get the biggest smile from them in response. We have no idea what these children are going through, and as a person teaching and protecting the next generation, I want all children to know someone "sees" them.

How Do You Affirm Yourself?

Baby, I will go get a mirror, look at myself, and say, "Oh, you look good today." Then I'll put on some lipstick, change my glasses, and throw on a cute outfit. Affirming conversation is essential as it helps me maintain my positivity and vibration. Even if I don't feel good, I know I am good.

Other ways I affirm myself are by listening to affirmations, sharing positive posts on social media, speaking words of encouragement, and listening to music. Music is the universal language that can make you want to dance or change your mood, feeling, and moment. Have you ever been mad as hell, but then your favorite song comes on? What happens? If you are like me, you change moods and start singing like you are performing at the Grammys. By the time your song is over, you are focusing on that new feeling, not the moment that made you mad. In addition to being a mood changer, music can also make you feel sexy and set the tone for intimacy. Have you ever heard a song that made you want to pick up the phone and make a call?

I love independent artist music, but I also enjoy hip-hop. Some of my favorite artists are Eric Roberson, Syleena Johnson, Keke Wyatt, and Raheem DeVaughn. I am a fan of not just good music but great lyrics. Eric Roberson has a song called "Lessons," and it's one of my favorites. It has beautiful lyrics and is an affirmation for me. He speaks about things I've been through but then reminds me that the lessons are bigger than the actions. Thus, helping me understand that I am not my pain, trauma, or a product of curses. I can rewrite the narrative and become who God has ordained me to be. The lessons are the blueprint to be better, not bitter.

Now that you know what I do to affirm myself, list some things you do to affirm yourself and your decisions.

Dr. Katrina R. Sparks

AFFIRMATIONS

As we reach the end of this book, I want to leave you with some powerful affirmations and reflection worksheets that you can complete daily to help you. Healing is a consistent and daily process that requires you to do the work and encourage yourself in order to achieve the desired outcome. As you know, it's easy to backslide and invite the old you back into your life, but we all know that is not what you want. So, as your sistahfriend in this season, allow me to speak life into you to encourage you.

Please know that even though I have gone through much of the healing process, I am still a work in process. I am not fully healed or whole, but I am better than I was ten years ago. So, I celebrate the progress and stay prepared and positive for what's to come. I do this by affirming myself daily, journaling, and completing worksheets or exercises that keep my mindset clear of distractions or self-doubt. Here are some of my favorite affirmations. I pray they encourage you as much as they have evolved me.

- I'm too blessed to be stressed.
- Today is a new day, and I'm choosing to be happy.
- My life is taking place right here, right now.
- I'm gifted with and surrounded by amazing friends and family.

- I opt to rise above negative feelings and ditch negative thoughts.
- I am resilient, strong, and brave. I cannot be destroyed.
- Nobody but me decides how I feel.
- When I lie down to sleep, everything is as it should be, and I rest content.
- I am in charge of my thoughts and don't judge myself.
- I accept and love myself wholly and thoroughly.

Now that you have read mine, I want you to write some of your own. Use the following space to speak life into you. Your inner self can't wait for you to encourage it.

_____

_____

_____

_____

_____

_____

_____

_____

_____

_____

_____

_____

_____

_____

_____

_____

_____

_____

_____

_____

_____

_____

_____

_____

_____

_____

_____

_____

Overall, healing through self-care is learning that it's okay to make time for ourselves. As much as we serve, work, and invest, we must know when enough is enough. We must understand when we need to take a timeout and check in on ourselves. I don't care how strong or reliable you are or how everyone leans on you; you have to consider this: *If I am no longer here, who will everyone run to?* As selfish as it may sound, sometimes you must function as if you are not here and do you. My last act of self-care was a trip to California. During my four days there, I enjoyed the sun and beach, and I got a colonic and blood analysis done. This trip wasn't just about my outer shell but my inner being. I needed complete restoration and rejuvenation. With indulging in tasty food and getting great sleep, I returned home feeling like a new woman.

There is nothing wrong with dating yourself, pampering yourself, having a lazy weekend with the cell phone off, taking walks in the park alone, or just locking yourself in the bathroom and enjoying a bath. You were not born to be burned out or overworked by life. You are supposed to enjoy it, as well. As I grow wiser, I have added myself to my calendar, and I take an hour or two for me. Nowadays, self-care for me looks like traveling, creating new memories and experiences, the beach, and simply doing what I love.

As you continue this journey, I challenge you to selfishly focus on yourself. Remember, you are no good to the world if you are no good as a person. Before we close this chapter, I would like you to write a letter of commitment to yourself, holding yourself accountable for the answers you have written in this book and the goals you have set for yourself. Many of us start the work and then stop before reaching our goal, but this season, we are striving for better. So, in the provided space, pen your official letter to yourself expressing what your better looks like. Once done, hang it on your mirror or wall so you can remind yourself daily. I believe in you and want nothing but the best for you. I will share my letter first, and you will write yours right after.

Dear Dr. Katrina R. Sparks,

Today, I am making a commitment to take my life back from my past. I am no longer what happened to me or what people have said about me. I am a child of God who has been promised life more abundantly. I am committed to getting better and removing the bitter so I can appreciate the rest of my life. I will no longer sit in pity or shame, allowing time to pass me by. Time is of the essence! And since I have more time behind me than ahead of me, I am no longer taking anything for granted. I promise to take care of myself because I have a responsibility to myself to live the best life possible and fulfill my purpose with love and integrity. I've seen what happens when I don't take care of myself and how it affects the people in my life. By committing to myself, I'm committing to the betterment of all.

I promise to be aware of the signs when I'm not taking care of myself. I will not be hard on myself or abuse myself in any way. I will take one step in the right direction to put the focus back on myself and commit to my journey. I know I need to slow down and be present, so I will commit to taking three deep breaths as a part of being there for myself. This will give me enough time to slow down and re-evaluate the situation. It is not my business how other people take this change. I must trust that others will have their own journeys. Some may realize how much they can do for themselves by not depending on me. Others may get angry and walk away. Then, there will be those who will be happy to see me make better choices for myself. No matter what the case, I need to do this for me. If I do it for anyone else, I will fail. This is my journey. I trust that whatever the result is with the people around me, it will be what is best for me.

I will be gentle with myself. I will make mistakes as I figure out what works and what doesn't, but I won't use that something isn't working as an excuse to give up. I will simply make a new commitment and move on. I understand that just because something works for someone else doesn't mean it will be the right fit for me. It is my job to customize my own self-

care program. The goal is to feel better about who I am, where I am, and how I am. I know this can only happen by taking care of myself, because no one else can know me if I don't know myself. I want to project to the world the magnificent person I am. Today, I commit to me.

With gratitude,

A Better Me

Now it's your turn. Take a deep breath and allow your words to flow. But, remember, whatever you write, own it and live by it.

Dear _____ **(insert your name),**

_____

_____

_____

_____

_____

_____

_____

_____

DR. KATRINA R. SPARKS

_____

_____

_____

_____

_____

_____

_____

_____

_____

_____

_____

_____

_____

_____

_____

_____

_____

_____

_____

_____

_____

_____

_____

_____

_____

_____

_____

_____

_____

_____

_____

_____

_____

With gratitude,

A Better Me

NOT BITTER, BETTER

Mommy, I did it! What a dream come true! Authoring this book is one of the things I've wanted to do for a long time now. I guess it's true what they say—"Life gets better after fifty." I remember when I started considering authoring this book. Right after my birthday and last journey to Africa, I encountered a spiritual awakening. I returned with a mission and started cleaning the house. From saying no to ending toxic relationships, I made my life about me. I wanted to focus on everything I had deprived myself of for years, and completing this project was one of them. So, if there is something you want to do, do it. Authoring this book was different than anything I have ever done, but mission accomplished, thanks to the support and help from my coach and friends. I also must add that authoring my story, creating and completing the assignments, and the whole journey itself were very therapeutic. It's one thing to talk about your issues, but writing about them and reading them over provides so much clarity. Being one with your mind and heart brings out everything you have been suppressing all these years.

Did you enjoy the book? What were some of the biggest "ah-ha" moments or takeaways you received from doing the assignments? My intention was to provide you with the necessary tools and strategies to help you identify what's within you that needs to be released. These tools are things I've used to propel me from unfulfilled Katrina to well-lived Dr. Sparks. I hope they helped you to discover the better you within, too.

THANK YOU!

I want to thank everyone who took the time to read my story with unconditional love and respect. It is my hope that you applied grace to your life and realized that none of us are perfect. We all have a story, and our testimony will move the culture and the next generation forward. I also hope you completed all the assignments and learned more about yourself. Even though I shared my truth, this project was written for your breakthrough. I am nothing more than a cheerleader who doesn't mind teaching you the routine of healing. Now, remember, healing will not happen overnight. I am in my fifties and still healing and discovering new things about myself. However, I must say the journey was beautiful. As you move forward to better, I want to challenge you to start living in the present. Stop harping on the past and "what had happened," and focus on what's coming. "There's a reason why your windshield is bigger than your rearview mirror. Where you're going is more important than where you came from," author unknown. That saying holds true because you can't drive forward while focusing on what's behind you.

Starting today, we will give ourselves permission to live, especially since we did the work yesterday to forgive ourselves. Today, I want you to reward yourself by sharing your goals, visions, hopes and dreams, love, and prayer for the person you are now choosing to become. She deserves to know what is ahead of her so she can plan accordingly to receive it while being ready for any shifts that life may bring. It is time to have what you always prayed for, what God ordained for you, and the ability to be grateful. See the good in what was intended for bad. Today, offer yourself the courage and permission to love yourself to no end. After you celebrate manifesting your goal list, I want you to have a wonderful day on purpose. Get your hair and nails done; get a manicure and pedicure; get a massage; get a gym membership; have a lunch date alone at the most expensive restaurant without worrying about the prices on the menu. Today, it is about celebrating and preparing for your life to come.

Allow today to be the start of your freedom. Get intentional about your next steps and prepare mentally, emotionally, and physically for the journey because I am here to warn you that the devil will get busy. Your happiness will insult him, thus causing him throw delays, detours, and trickery your way. However, his weapons will never gain traction if you prepare as you execute. They will just become steps to your elevation that will get you to your destiny faster!

Remember, you are no longer bitter.
You are better! Move in peace and gratitude!

Prayer for Gratitude

Dear God,

Thank you for your amazing power and work in my life. Thank you for your goodness and blessings over me. Thank you for supplying my mind and heart with hope through even the toughest times, strengthening me for your purposes. Thank you for helping me see that there is glory and mercy in life's unexpected struggles. That I, too, am a conqueror, and even though weapons will form, they will never prosper. Thank you for always being with us, even when I refuse to trust your presence. Thank you for never quitting on a sinner like me, for you know my imperfections but never use them against me. Thank you for your forgiveness and the ability to call me your child still. Thank you for your incredible sacrifice so that we might have freedom and life everlasting. Help us set our eyes and hearts on you, moving in a purpose of readiness and optimism. Renew our spirits; fill us with your peace and joy. We love you, and we need you this day and every day. We give you all the praise, all the glory, and all the honor, for You alone are worthy! In Jesus' Name, Amen.

Thank you for taking this
journey with me!

Peace & Blessings

Resources

Autism
Autism Speaks ~ www.autismspeaks.org
Autism Parenting Magazine ~
www.autismparentingmagazine.com
Autism Society ~ www.autism-society.org
The National Autism Center ~
www.nationalautismcenter.org

Parenting
The ABA Parent Toolbox ~ www.theabaparent.com
Mommy Poppins ~ www.mommypoppins.com

Therapy
Boris Lawrence Henson Foundation ~
https://borislhensonfoundation.org/
Black Girls Journal ~
https://www.blackgirlsjournal.co/shop

Travel
Sky Scanner ~ https://www.skyscanner.com/
The Smart Traveler Enrollment Program ~
https://www.smartraveller.gov.au/
Groupon ~ https://www.groupon.com/
Travel Pirates ~ https://www.travelpirates.com/

Hopper ~ https://hopper.com/
Book It ~ http://www.bookittravel.com/
Air BNB ~ https://www.airbnb.com/
Travel Zoo ~ https://www.travelzoo.com/
Travelocity ~ https://www.travelocity.com/
Expedia ~ https://www.expedia.com/
Kayak ~ https://www.kayak.com/
Sanders ~ https://hotelsanders.com/

Author Bio

Dr. Katrina R. Sparks is a mother, daughter, author, and educator. The foundation of who she is, is grounded in a determination to defy the odds and an unyielding willingness to fight through life's challenges. These traits have resulted in Dr. Sparks being the epitome of today's immensely complex and powerfully spirited woman.

Born in Westbury, New York, Dr. Sparks' impeccable credentials exemplify a current crop of African American women who have met the challenges of modern life in America. Dr. Sparks completed her undergraduate work at Herbert Lehman College, where she majored in African American Studies with a concentration in Early Childhood Education, and she graduated with a Bachelor of Arts degree in 1993. She went on to further her education by earning her first Master's degree in Special Education from Long Island University/Brooklyn

Campus in 1998. She earned a second Master's degree in School Administration and Supervision from Massachusetts College of Liberal Arts at North Adams, MA, in 2002 and a third Master's from Argosy University in Educational Specialist/Educational Leadership in 2003. In 2007, Dr. Sparks earned a Doctorate of Philosophy in Professional Studies in Education from Capella University. She recently got accepted into The Chicago School of Professional Psychology and its Post Master's Certificate in Applied Behavior Analysis Program.

Dr. Katrina R. Sparks is an educator whose area of concentration is in Special Education. She has taught in the areas of development and instruction of the special needs population for over 29 years and is currently employed in the capacity of a Special Education Teacher. In addition, Dr. Sparks works as a consultant in Early Intervention and CPSE (Committee of Pre-school Education). Her responsibilities include Teacher of Speech and Hearing Handicapped, S.E.I.T (Special Education Itinerant Teacher), ABA Applied Behavior Analysis, and Education Evaluator.

The consummate educator, Dr. Sparks holds permanent certifications in Special Education, Teacher of the Speech and Hearing Impaired, Adult Education and Literacy (GED Preparation) Instructor, School District

Administration/ Supervision (SDA), and School Administration/ Supervision (SAS).

Among her many accomplishments and acknowledgements are:

- Being featured in *Essence Magazine* in 2006 in an article recognizing women who turned personal interests into a profitable endeavor.
- Being a two-time feature in the *Culvert Chronicles* in 2009.
- Being a two-time feature in the *New York Amsterdam Newspaper*.
- A published dissertation entitled "The Individualized Education Plan: Parent Perspectives on the Feasibility and Effectiveness of the Individualized Educational Plan.
- A proud member of Zeta Phi Beta Sorority Inc., initiated in the spring of 1998 through Nu Psi Zeta in Peekskill, New York.
- Former Kappa Epsilon Zeta Chapter member in the Bronx, New York, where she held the position of 3rd Anti-Basileus and founded the Archonette Auxiliary Club.
- 2nd Anti-Basileus of Zeta Phi Beta Sorority Inc., Gamma Alpha Sigma Zeta Chapter, Ghana.

- Founding 2nd Vice-Chair of the National Council of Black Women, Metro New York Chapter.
- Currently 1st Anti-Basileus of Zeta Phi Beta Sorority Inc., Gamma Alpha Sigma Zeta Chapter, Ghana.
- A member of The National Association of Black Educators (NABSE).